Hillary RODHAM CLINTON

Biography®

Hillary RODHAM CLINTON

JoAnn Bren Guernsey

Lerner Publications Company
Minneapolis

Copyright © 2005 by Lerner Publications Company

This book is available in two editions:
Library binding by Lerner Publications Company,
 a division of Lerner Publishing Group
Soft cover by First Avenue Editions,
 an imprint of Lerner Publishing Group
241 First Avenue North
Minneapolis, MN 55401 U.S.A.

Website address: www.lernerbooks.com

Library of Congress Cataloging-in-Publication Data

Guernsey, JoAnn Bren.
    Hillary Rodham Clinton / by JoAnn Bren Guernsey.
      p.   cm. — (A&E biography)
    Includes bibliographical references and index.
    ISBN: 0–8225–2372–8 (lib.bdg. : alk. paper)
    ISBN: 0–8225–9613–X (pbk : alk. paper)
    1. Clinton, Hillary Rodham—Juvenile literature. 2. Presidents' spouses—United States—Biography—Juvenile literature. 3. Legislators—United States—Biography—Juvenile literature. 4. Women legislators—United States—Biography—Juvenile literature. 5. United States. Congress. Senate—Biography—Juvenile literature. I. Title. II. Series: Biography (Lerner Publications Company)
    E887.C55G838 2005
    328.73'092—dc22   2004021746

Manufactured in the United States of America
1 2 3 4 5 6 – JR – 10 09 08 07 06 05

CONTENTS

Hillary Clinton shares a moment with her husband, Bill, before announcing her candidacy for the U.S. Senate in February 2000.

INTRODUCTION

Hillary Rodham Clinton faced a big decision. The year was 1999. For more than six years, she had been First Lady of the United States—the wife of President Bill Clinton, a Democrat. She had lived in the White House with Bill and their daughter, Chelsea. She had advised her husband on pressing political problems and defended him from political opponents. But Hillary Rodham Clinton was more than just her husband's helper. During Bill Clinton's presidency, she had met with famous world leaders. She had worked on important government projects. She had recommended major reforms of the nation's health care system. And long before her husband had become president, Clinton had had a distinguished career as a lawyer.

She was a powerful, intelligent woman who held an important place in American society. But with Bill Clinton's presidential term ending in early 2001, her job as First Lady would end as well. What would Hillary Clinton do afterward?

Many people wanted to hire her. She had job offers from colleges, big corporations, TV shows, and charitable organizations. All these groups were eager to work with such a well-known and accomplished person with big-name connections in government. The Democratic Party wanted Hillary Clinton too. Democratic leaders began to ask: Would she consider running for the U.S.

Senate? Daniel Moynihan, a longtime senator from New York, had announced his upcoming retirement. Would Clinton consider running for his seat as a U.S. senator from New York in 2000?

At first, Clinton didn't take the idea seriously. After all, she wasn't a native New Yorker. She would have to move to New York before she could run for office there. She had never held elected public office before. And her Republican opponent was likely to be Rudolph Giuliani, the popular New York City mayor. Even if Clinton were interested in the job—which she wasn't, she insisted—it seemed unlikely that she could beat Giuliani.

But the Democratic leadership wouldn't give up. One by one, prominent Democrats began to mention her name as their favorite candidate. Finally, Senator Moynihan himself added his support. He told an NBC correspondent that if Hillary Clinton were to run for the Senate, "She'd be welcome and she'd win."

Pressured by her fellow Democrats, Clinton agreed to at least consider the idea. On the negative side, she dreaded a long, exhausting political campaign. She knew the Republican Party was sure to launch mean-spirited campaign ads against her. And since she didn't yet live in New York, she knew she'd be called a carpetbagger—an outsider who comes to a new area and meddles in its politics. Still, the idea of joining the U.S. Senate—the most powerful group of lawmakers in the United States—was tempting. Clinton thought it over. She talked about it with Bill and her close friends and advisers.

On March 4, 1999, Clinton was scheduled to speak to a group of young female athletes in New York City. Along with retired tennis champion Billie Jean King, she was there to promote an HBO film called *Dare to Compete*, about women in sports. A teenage basketball player named Sofia Totti introduced Clinton to the crowd. As Sofia shook Clinton's hand, she also whispered in her ear: "Dare to compete, Mrs. Clinton. Dare to compete."

Sofia's words hit home. After the event, Clinton realized that, like the young female athletes, she *would* dare to compete. She *would* run for the U.S. Senate. She later reflected, "All over the United States and in scores of countries, I had spoken out about the importance of women participating in politics and government, seeking elective office and using the power of their own voices to shape public policy and chart their nations' futures. How could I pass up an opportunity to do the same?"

The decision was made. After a "listening tour" to touch base with New York voters and a move to an old farmhouse in Chappaqua, north of New York City, Hillary Clinton formally declared her candidacy in February 2000. In mid-May, at their state convention, New York's Democrats officially named her their candidate for the Senate. As her job as First Lady wound down, Hillary Rodham Clinton set forth into uncharted territory.

Hillary Rodham grew up in this house in Park Ridge, Illinois.

Chapter **ONE**

A YOUNG ACTIVIST

HILLARY DIANE RODHAM WAS BORN ON OCTOBER 26, 1947, at Edgewater Hospital on the north side of Chicago, Illinois. She grew up in a stone-and-brick house on the corner of Wisner and Elm streets in Park Ridge, a middle-class Chicago suburb.

Her father, Hugh Rodham, had started his career as a curtain salesman at the Columbia Lace Company in Chicago. Dorothy Howell Rodham, Hillary's mother, met Hugh when she applied for a secretarial job at the company in 1937. Dorothy and Hugh were married in 1942. After serving in the navy during World War II (1939–1945), Hugh Rodham opened his own drapery-making business, Rodrik Fabrics, in Chicago.

Like most women of this era, Dorothy stayed home to raise children. Hillary had two younger brothers: Hugh Jr., born three years after Hillary, and Anthony (Tony), born four years after Hugh. Dorothy was proud of her work as a full-time housewife and mother. Hillary remembers her as a "woman in perpetual motion, making the beds, washing the dishes, and putting dinner on the table precisely at six o'clock." At the same time, Dorothy developed and passed on to her children what would later be called feminist ideals. She said, "I was determined that no daughter of mine was going to have to go through the agony of being afraid to say what she had on her mind." Hillary added, "My parents gave me my belief in working hard, doing well in school, and not being limited by the fact that I was a little girl."

Hillary learned early in life to assert herself. A neighborhood family, the O'Callaghans, had a daughter named Suzy, who often bullied other children. Hillary was a small four-year-old when she became the frequent target of Suzy's fists. After being hit, Hillary would run home sobbing. One day her mother made an announcement. "There's no room in this house for cowards. You're going to have to stand up to her. The next time she hits you, I want you to hit her back."

It wasn't long before Hillary faced Suzy again, and the confrontation soon attracted a circle of curious neighborhood kids. Nobody expected what happened next. Hillary—eyes closed—threw out her fist, knocking Suzy to the ground. The other children's mouths dropped open in awe. Hillary raced home, delighted with her triumph. She exclaimed to her mother that she was now tough enough to play with the boys.

The neighborhood in Park Ridge was full of families with young children. "There must have been forty or fifty children within a four-block radius of our house, and within four years of Hillary's age. They were all together, all the time, a big extended family...lots of playing and competition. She held her own at cops and robbers, hide and seek, chase and run," Hillary's mother recalled.

Hillary took piano lessons and ballet lessons. She played in a girls' softball league in summer and joined in pickup football and field hockey games with her brothers and other children. Ice-skating, swimming, and bike riding were other favorite activities. Hillary was a Brownie and then a Girl Scout. She took part in Scout parades, food drives, and cookie sales, and she earned almost every merit badge possible. At the age of nine, doctors found that Hillary was nearsighted, and she got her first pair of eyeglasses.

Along with friends, Hillary went to see movies at the Pickwick Theater. The whole family liked to go to Wrigley Field in Chicago to root for the Chicago Cubs baseball team. Every August they went to Hugh's father's cottage on Lake Winola in the Pocono Mountains of Pennsylvania.

SCHOOL OF HARD KNOCKS

The Rodham family was financially secure. Hugh Rodham owned a successful business, and he always drove
a Cadillac—a high-priced car. But the Rodham children
were not pampered. Hugh routinely had the children
rake leaves, cut the grass, pull weeds, and shovel snow.
They all worked at his drapery shop when he needed
extra help. He'd occasionally give the children some
spending money but never a regular allowance. "They
eat and sleep for free," he once grumbled. "We're not
going to pay them for it as well!"

Hugh and Dorothy had grown up during the Great
Depression, a period of economic hardship in the
1930s. Both their families had scraped and struggled
to get by. Dorothy had had a particularly harsh childhood—she had been sent to live with her grandparents at the age of eight and was working full-time by
aged fourteen. As parents, Hugh and Dorothy wanted
their children to appreciate their good fortune. On
trips into downtown Chicago, they often drove
through run-down neighborhoods so the children
could see poverty up close.

Hillary felt sorry for children who weren't as well off
as she was. When she was still in elementary school,
she grew concerned about the children of Mexican
migrant (traveling) workers, poor laborers who picked
crops on farms near her home. Hillary decided to raise
money and gather clothing for the workers' families.
To raise funds, she organized carnivals and sports

Hillary's work on behalf of others began when she was a young girl. She is pictured above, first row, far right, with her sixth grade classmates.

tournaments with neighborhood kids, charging a small fee to spectators. Later, she organized a babysitting service for the migrant children. She also raised money for the United Way and other charities.

The biggest responsibility for the Rodham children was schoolwork. Hillary always earned top grades at school. At report card time, Hillary remembers her mother praising her straight-A record. But her father made a snide remark. "You must go to a pretty easy school," he said when he saw her report card.

Early on, Hillary started thinking about a career. When she was fourteen, she wrote to the National Aeronautics and Space Administration (NASA). She was interested in the newly created space program, and she asked in her letter what she had to do to become an astronaut. An official at NASA soon answered. "We are not accepting girls as astronauts," he wrote. Hillary remembers being furious with this reply.

POLITICAL AWAKENINGS

Hillary was active at the First United Methodist Church, located in a redbrick building not far from the Rodham house. She attended Bible school, Sunday school, and a youth group there. When Hillary was in ninth grade, the Reverend Donald Jones arrived from New York City to become the church's new youth minister.

For several years, Hillary attended Jones's Methodist Youth Fellowship sessions. Jones called these classes the University of Life. During the sessions, he talked about God, justice, poverty, music, and art. At this "university," Hillary and the other teenagers also learned about writers such as e. e. cummings and Fyodor Dostoyevsky, musician Bob Dylan, and French filmmaker Francois Truffaut. Jones introduced the students to Pablo Picasso's *Guernica*, a painting that addresses the horrors of war, and led them in discussions about war and peace.

All the teenagers in the youth group were white and middle class. Jones wanted them to learn about people from other backgrounds, so he took them to churches on Chicago's South Side. There, they met and talked with street kids, gang members, African Americans, and Hispanics.

In 1962 the group traveled to Orchestra Hall in Chicago to hear a speech by civil rights leader Martin Luther King Jr. King talked about racial injustice, poverty, and the struggle to end segregation (the separation of races) in the United States. After the speech, Jones took his group backstage and introduced the teenagers, including Hillary, to Dr. King. At the time, Hillary was only dimly aware of the civil rights movement and other protest movements taking place across the United States. King's words began to open her eyes to the national scene.

By 1962 Dr. Martin Luther King Jr., right, had been working tirelessly toward equal rights for all citizens for many years.

Hillary, seated, front, became student council chairperson during her senior year in high school.

At high school—first Maine East High and later Maine South—Hillary earned high grades every year. She joined the National Honor Society and organized the junior prom. She also made her first venture into politics in those years. She successfully ran for student council and junior class vice president. She also served on a student group called the Cultural Values Committee, which tried to promote unity, respect, and understanding among students from different social backgrounds. During her senior year, she ran for student government president but lost the election.

Hillary was interested in national politics as well. Her father was a Republican, and at first, Hillary followed in his political footsteps. The Republican Party believed in free enterprise—the idea that private businesses should be able to operate with very little government interference. The Republicans didn't think government should try to solve social problems such as poverty or racial discrimination. In the 1950s and 1960s, the Republicans greatly distrusted the Communist Soviet Union and worried about Communism spreading to many nations throughout the world. (Communists favor a state-run economy, with no private property or free enterprise.)

Hillary thought the Republican ideas made sense. She joined a group called the Young Republicans and an anti-Communist club. During her senior year, in 1964, she campaigned for presidential candidate Barry Goldwater, a conservative Republican. As a

Quotes from Barry Goldwater's acceptance speech for the Republican nomination adorn this button from his 1964 presidential campaign.

"Goldwater girl," she wore a cowboy costume and a straw hat with the slogan "AuH$_2$O," which stood for "gold water." (The letters come from chemistry's table of elements, which lists the chemical substances that make up all matter.)

Her civics teacher, Jerry Baker, organized a mock presidential debate, with students playing the part of the two presidential candidates: Goldwater for the Republicans and President Lyndon Johnson for the Democrats. Baker wanted students to open their minds to opposing political viewpoints, so he had Ellen Press, a girl who normally backed the Democrats, play the part of Goldwater. He had Hillary, a Young Republican, play the part of Johnson. To prepare for the debate, Hillary recalls, "I immersed myself—for the first time—in President Johnson's Democratic positions on civil rights, health care, poverty, and foreign policy." As she became more and more familiar with the issues, she began to have a few doubts about her Republican leanings.

During her senior year, Hillary considered her options for college. Encouraged by two teachers, she applied to (and was accepted by) Smith and Wellesley, both women's colleges in Massachusetts. She never visited the campuses, but she talked to alumni and students and reviewed each school's promotional literature. She chose Wellesley, in part because the campus had a small lake, Lake Waban, that reminded her of Lake Winola in Pennsylvania.

Hillary graduated from high school with many honors, including a social science award. Of the 566 students in her class, she stood in the top 5 percent. In the fall of 1965, Hillary and her parents drove from Illinois to Massachusetts, where Hillary would begin her freshman year at Wellesley.

Hillary Rodham in 1965

Chapter **TWO**

AN EXPLOSION
OF IDEAS

WHEN HILLARY RODHAM ARRIVED AT WELLESLEY College, in the charming New England town of Wellesley, Massachusetts, she found herself at a school steeped in tradition. One of seven top-level women's colleges called the Seven Sisters, Wellesley had been founded in 1870. In 1965, when Rodham arrived, Wellesley students followed a strict code of conduct. They had to wear skirts to dinner. They had to obey a curfew (be in their dorm rooms by a certain hour). Young men weren't allowed to visit them in their rooms except on Sunday afternoons.

Almost all the Wellesley students were white. Some belonged to the nation's most prominent and wealthiest families. Rodham met young women who had graduated from private boarding schools, lived in Europe, and spoke foreign languages fluently. The only time Rodham had left the country was to see Niagara Falls in Canada. The school was "all very rich and fancy and very intimidating to my way of thinking," she remembers.

Rodham felt out of place at first, but she quickly adjusted to her new surroundings. She moved into Stone-Davis, a grand old dormitory on the shores of Lake Waban. She jumped into campus activities, joining the school's Young Republicans club and becoming its president. On weekends she dated young men, mostly students from nearby Harvard and other elite colleges. On Sundays she attended services at the local Methodist church.

A NEW AMERICAN REVOLUTION

Hillary Rodham and her Wellesley classmates enjoyed a serene life on campus. But outside the sheltered college environment, the United States was undergoing big changes. In early 1965, Martin Luther King Jr. had led dramatic—but nonviolent—antisegregation marches in Alabama. Later that year, protesters had arrived in Washington, D.C., to speak out against U.S. involvement in the Vietnam War, which was raging in Southeast Asia. Groups such as Students for a Democratic Society began to question U.S. government policies regarding war, business, politics, and race relations. Women began to question their traditional, limited roles as mothers and housekeepers. Popular musicians—artists such as Bob Dylan and Joan Baez—sang about peace and justice.

A political and cultural revolution had started to sweep the nation, especially on college campuses. Soon even the well-brought-up, wealthy young women of Wellesley were talking about changing society. Many abandoned their prim hairdos and nicely pressed outfits and adopted the newly fashionable "flower child" look, complete with bell-bottom blue jeans, headbands, peace symbols, and tie-dyed T-shirts.

In the mid-1960s, the casual flower child look became popular. Rodham, like many young people, adopted the new look with ease.

Hillary Rodham began to read a magazine called *motive*. Published by the Methodist Church, the magazine examined the civil rights struggle, the Vietnam War, and other timely issues. She discussed and debated current affairs with her classmates and professors. She took courses in sociology, philosophy, and psychology. She eventually majored in political science. "My mind exploded when I got to Wellesley," Rodham remembered.

About a year after arriving at college, she abandoned the Republican beliefs she had once shared with her father. She no longer thought that government should ignore social issues and let big business operate as it pleased. She thought instead that government should help people—all people: black and white, young and old, rich and poor, male and female—to improve their own lives. She resigned from the Young Republicans.

Rodham began to learn everything she could about the Vietnam War. The United States had entered the war to help South Vietnam, which was fighting a takeover by Communist North Vietnam. Many students, including Hillary Rodham, thought the United States should withdraw from the war and let the Vietnamese people decide their own future. But the U.S. government was determined not to let South Vietnam fall to the Communists. The government sent thousands and thousands of soldiers to Vietnam. The more soldiers it sent, the more other young people in the

Hundreds of thousands of antiwar demonstrators gather in Washington, D.C., in the late 1960s.

United States protested against the war. Some young men who were drafted into (selected for) the military refused to fight.

During her junior year, in 1967, Rodham wanted to do her part to stop U.S. involvement in the Vietnam War. She joined the campaign of Eugene McCarthy—a Democrat and an antiwar senator from Minnesota. McCarthy was trying to win the 1968 Democratic presidential nomination. On weekends, Rodham and a few friends would drive more than an hour to New Hampshire to stuff envelopes and do other work for the McCarthy campaign.

Early in 1968, Rodham engaged in yet another political campaign—her own race for student body president. After campaigning enthusiastically in the Wellesley dorms, she beat out two opponents for the job.

PAINFUL LESSONS

The year 1968 was difficult for the United States. The Vietnam War continued to rage in Asia. Antiwar protests got larger and larger. The movement for civil rights became more vocal and sometimes violent. Then, on April 4, 1968, a gunman killed civil rights leader Dr. Martin Luther King Jr. in Memphis, Tennessee.

Since meeting Martin Luther King as a teenager, Rodham had spent many hours reading about King, his tactics of nonviolent protest, and his work to achieve equality for African Americans. She, like other Americans, was saddened by the assassination. Rodham joined a crowd in downtown Boston, Massachusetts, to peacefully protest the event and to mourn King's death.

Two months after King's assassination, Senator Robert F. Kennedy (also seeking the Democratic presidential nomination) was shot and killed in Los Angeles, California. To compound the tragedy, Robert Kennedy was the brother of President John F. Kennedy, who had been assassinated five years before. To many Americans, the United States seemed to be falling into chaos. The nation went into mourning once more.

Distressed about the killings but nevertheless hopeful, Hillary Rodham left Wellesley for a summer internship in Washington, D.C. The internship would give her firsthand experience with the workings of the U.S. government. But her plans had taken a strange twist. When she had arrived at Wellesley, she had been a Republican. So the professor in charge of the internship program scheduled her to intern for a group of Republican congresspeople. Rodham protested the assignment—after all, she had lately become a Democrat—but the job couldn't be changed.

Rodham knew she could learn plenty from the Republicans as well as the Democrats. In Washington that summer, she talked about the Vietnam War with members of Congress. She met important government officials, including Congressman Gerald Ford (later U.S. president). She even attended the Republican National Convention in Miami, Florida, where Richard Nixon won the presidential nomination.

When her internship ended in August, Rodham returned to Park Ridge to visit her family for a few weeks before returning to school. The Democrats were holding their presidential convention in downtown Chicago that summer. Thousands of demonstrators had gathered in nearby Grant Park to protest U.S. involvement in the Vietnam War. Rodham and a friend from high school, Betsy Johnson, wanted to witness the demonstration in person, so they took the train from Park Ridge to downtown Chicago.

They were not prepared for what they saw at the park. The protest had turned into a violent confrontation between demonstrators and the police.

Police and antiwar protesters clash outside the Democratic National Convention in Chicago, Illinois, in 1968.

"You could smell the tear gas before you saw the lines of police," Rodham remembered. "In the crowd behind us, someone screamed profanities and threw a rock, which just missed us. Betsy and I scrambled to get away as the police charged the crowd with nightsticks."

Rodham was upset by the violence. She was convinced that rock throwing and tear gas would never solve political problems. The best ways to change government or society, she believed, involved nonviolent protest—like that used by Martin Luther King

Jr.—as well as "working within the system." People who wanted change, she thought, needed to run for office, take jobs in law and government, and work peacefully within community organizations to achieve their goals. For her own part, Rodham wanted to work within the system by becoming a lawyer.

SENIORITIS

By her senior year at Wellesley, Hillary Rodham was a confident young woman. She was a top student and class president, with a long list of accomplishments to her name. So when she applied to law school at Yale and Harvard—the best programs in the nation—she was quickly accepted by both universities. When trying to choose between the two schools, Rodham met a Harvard professor. "We don't need any more women at Harvard," he coldly told her. That comment soured her on Harvard, so she chose Yale.

May 31, 1969, was graduation day for the Wellesley seniors. Their official commencement speaker would be Massachusetts senator Edward Brooke. But someone else was scheduled to speak as well: class president Hillary Rodham. In front of her father (her mother was home sick), teachers, and classmates, Rodham took her turn at the podium. The speech she made—written with the help of classmates— sharply criticized the administration of Richard Nixon, who had won the 1968 presidential election. She urged her fellow students to continue to protest

Rodham, second from left, on graduation day at Wellesley College in 1969.

against the government—but to do so constructively. Her words were hopeful and stirring. "The challenge now is to practice politics as the art of making what appears to be impossible, possible," she said.

To Rodham's surprise, the speech attracted attention nationwide. *Life* magazine published an article about her, along with her photograph. Reporters called her mother at home in Park Ridge. Many young people were speaking out at the time—criticizing the war, calling for women's rights, fighting for social justice. But Hillary Rodham stood out from the crowd. In calling her fellow students to action, observers said, Hillary Rodham had spoken for an entire generation.

Rodham continued to be active in politics while she attended Yale Law School.

Chapter **THREE**

FROM YALE TO ARKANSAS

HILLARY RODHAM ENTERED YALE LAW SCHOOL IN the fall of 1969. Like Wellesley, Yale was a school steeped in wealth and tradition. But the campus was alive with new ideas in 1969. Like college students around the country, Yale students were active in the civil rights movement, the antiwar movement, and the women's movement.

During her first year, 1969–1970, Rodham focused intently on her law school classes. But there were many distractions. Some of her classmates demonstrated in support of the Black Panthers, a radical African American political organization. Even more students demonstrated against the expansion of the Vietnam War from Vietnam into neighboring Cambodia. Rodham helped lead a large meeting, where Yale law students voted to take a stand against the war. But Rodham didn't agree with student protesters who used violence. She was determined to change society by working within the system.

Because of all the press attention from her Wellesley commencement speech, Rodham received many invitations to speak at political events. The League of Women Voters invited her to speak at a meeting on May 7, 1970. At the meeting in Washington, D.C., Rodham argued against the expansion of the Vietnam War. She also met the meeting's keynote speaker, Marian Wright Edelman, a civil rights advocate.

Edelman was starting an antipoverty organization in Washington, D.C., and Rodham asked for a summer job with the group. Rodham could have the job, Edelman replied, but the group had no money to pay her a salary. Undeterred, Rodham applied for and won a grant (an award of money) from a civil rights organization. The grant enabled her to live and work in Washington even without a salary.

Rodham's work that summer involved doing research on the education and health of the children of migrant farmworkers. This research focused her attention on the plight of children living in poverty. When she returned to Yale in the fall, she decided to make children's rights the focus of her law school studies.

A HANDSOME STRANGER

In the fall of 1970, a young man arrived on the Yale campus. He had just returned from Oxford University in Great Britain, where he had been a Rhodes Scholar—winner of a prestigious academic award. He was a tall, charming Arkansan with a full beard and curly brown hair. He was William Jefferson Clinton, who went by the name of Bill.

Toward the end of the school year, in the spring of 1971, Bill Clinton was talking with a friend in the law school library when someone distracted him. A young woman wearing a flannel shirt and thick glasses was reading at the other end of the room. He couldn't stop staring at her. When she looked up from her book, she

Bill Clinton, center, and two friends during Clinton's last year at Oxford University

noticed him watching her, and she stared back. Finally, she shut her book, walked down to where Clinton sat, and said, "If you're going to keep looking at me, and I'm going to keep looking back, we might as well be introduced. I'm Hillary Rodham."

In fact, Hillary Rodham and Bill Clinton already knew about each other. She had seen him on campus and asked friends about him. She thought he was handsome and intriguing. He had seen her speak in class, and he knew about her news-making speech at the Wellesley commencement several years earlier. He thought she was magnetic and brilliant. He called her "the greatest thing on two legs."

Before long, the two were dating. But as the relationship turned more serious, both Rodham and Clinton wondered whether they could have a future together. She wanted to work as an attorney after law school, focusing on children's rights and other social causes, preferably in a big city. He had different goals altogether. "I'm going back to Arkansas, and I'm going to be governor" Clinton boldly told a lawyer who asked about his career plans. Of course, Clinton was just boasting. He knew he couldn't start his political career at the top of state government. But he was definitely set on holding political office.

During the summer and fall of 1972, Rodham and Clinton moved to Texas to work on the presidential campaign of Democratic senator George McGovern. Rodham worked in San Antonio, trying to register

Presidential candidate McGovern greets supporters. McGovern lost the 1972 election to Richard Nixon by a wide margin, winning a majority of votes in only Massachusetts and the District of Columbia.

Hispanic voters. Clinton ran McGovern's state campaign headquarters in Austin. When the election arrived in November, McGovern made a poor showing. He was soundly defeated by his Republican opponent, President Richard Nixon.

Normally, law school at Yale lasts three years, but Rodham stayed for one extra year. She took a special course of study at the Yale Child Study Center. There, she took part in research on child development. At the same time, she helped several professors write a book on children and the law, she helped the Yale–New

Haven Hospital draft guidelines for dealing with abused children, and she worked with foster children and foster parents at the New Haven Legal Services office.

Both Hillary Rodham and Bill Clinton finished their studies at Yale in the spring of 1973. Then they traveled to Great Britain, where they visited galleries, cathedrals, and historic ruins. On this trip, in the Lake District of northwestern England, Clinton asked Rodham to marry him. She loved him, but she wasn't sure about making a lifetime promise to him. She told him she wasn't ready for marriage.

CAREER PATHS

When the summer ended, Clinton and Rodham went separate ways. As planned, Clinton returned to Arkansas to prepare for a career in politics. He took a teaching job at the University of Arkansas Law School in Fayetteville, but he also began work on his first political campaign—a run for Congress. Rodham moved to Cambridge, Massachusetts. There, she took a job as a staff attorney for the Children's Defense Fund (CDF), a new organization created by Marian Wright Edelman. Although living more than a thousand miles apart, Rodham and Clinton kept in frequent touch by letters and phone. He came to visit her at Thanksgiving, and she visited him at Christmas.

In late 1973, the House Judiciary Committee (part of the House of Representatives) was putting together a team to investigate President Nixon. In an incident called Watergate, Nixon and his staff were accused of trying to win the 1972 election by using burglary, wiretapping, and spying against their Democratic opponents, then covering up their crimes. The head of the investigation team asked a colleague to recommend some sharp young lawyers to join his staff. The colleague recommended Hillary Rodham and Bill Clinton, along with two other recent Yale Law School graduates.

The job would involve long hours, low pay, and a move to Washington, D.C. Clinton was busy with his run for Congress, so he turned down the offer. But Rodham was intrigued by the idea. Like other Americans, she was upset that the president was suspected of wrongdoing. She also knew that the Watergate investigation would be a historic case—no president had ever been accused of such serious crimes before. Rodham jumped at the chance to be part of history.

In January 1974, Rodham joined the Watergate investigation team. The group's goal was to gather evidence that could impeach Nixon—in other words, charge him with a serious crime. But in August, before the full case could be brought against him, Nixon resigned from the presidency. He knew he would be found guilty, and he knew the American people had lost faith in him.

With Nixon's resignation, Rodham's job in Washington, D.C., ended. She sifted through job offers from law firms in Washington, New York, and Chicago. She was at a critical point in her career. Finally, she made

Rodham, center, and other lawyers discuss bringing impeachment charges against President Nixon in January 1974.

a difficult decision—one that shocked and dismayed her friends. She decided to move to Fayetteville, Arkansas. She accepted a job teaching criminal law at the University of Arkansas Law School, the same school where Bill Clinton was teaching.

"Are you out of your mind," said Rodham's friend Sara Ehrman when she heard the news. "Why on earth would you throw away your future?" Arkansas was a poor, rural state with a total population of about one-quarter that of New York City. Why would

Rodham want to live in sleepy Fayetteville when she could have her pick of high-paying, high-powered jobs in a big city? The answer was simple: Hillary Rodham loved Bill Clinton. She had decided to follow her heart to Arkansas.

A banner in Hot Springs, Arkansas, shows support for
Bill Clinton's 1974 congressional campaign.

Chapter **FOUR**

First Lady of Arkansas

FAYETTEVILLE IS A SMALL COLLEGE TOWN IN THE Ozark Mountains. It has hilly, tree-lined streets and lovely Victorian houses. Hillary Rodham arrived in town in August 1974. She rented a three-bedroom house and jumped into her teaching job with her usual energy and commitment. By the fall of 1974, Bill Clinton's campaign for Congress was in full swing. During her spare time, Rodham helped at campaign headquarters. But when the election came in November, Clinton lost by a small margin.

As a law school professor, Rodham was demanding of and well respected by her students. In addition to teaching, she set up a university program to provide legal services for people in Fayetteville who could not afford lawyers. When the school year ended, Rodham took a summer trip to visit friends and family in Chicago, Boston, New York, and Washington, D.C. When she returned, Bill Clinton picked her up at the airport. But instead of taking her home, he drove up to a small redbrick house that she had admired earlier in the summer. He stopped the car. Much to Rodham's surprise, Clinton announced that he had bought the house, and he added: "Now you'd better marry me because I can't live in it by myself."

This time, she accepted his proposal. They didn't bother with a long engagement or elaborate wedding plans. They had a small wedding ceremony in the living room of the new house in October. Only close friends and family attended the ceremony. Then a larger group gathered in a friend's backyard for a reception. Nearly everyone had a good time at the party, but Bill Clinton's mother, Virginia Kelley, was upset. Before the wedding, Bill had told her that Hillary would not be taking the last name Clinton after she got married. She would keep the name Hillary Rodham. At the time, this was an unusual decision, and Clinton's traditional mother wasn't happy about it.

In another break with tradition, the couple didn't take a typical honeymoon. Instead, Bill, Hillary, Hillary's parents, and Hillary's two brothers all took a vacation in Acapulco, Mexico, for ten days. "It was a honeymoon for six!" Hillary's brother Tony remarked.

Picking up the Pace

The newlyweds' life in peaceful Fayetteville came to an end in late 1976, when Bill Clinton was elected to serve as Arkansas's attorney general—the state's chief law officer. This change required the couple to move to the Arkansas capital of Little Rock. Therefore, Rodham had to give up her teaching job in Fayetteville. Searching around for another position, she signed on with the Rose Law Firm, the most well-respected law practice in Arkansas.

She quickly became known as an energetic and determined lawyer. She worked on a variety of cases, including many involving the protection of children. Bill Clinton, meanwhile, was moving up fast. A popular attorney general, he decided the time was right to make a run for governor of Arkansas. He hit the campaign trail in early 1978. Attractive and well spoken, with a magnetic personality, he easily beat out four other candidates to win the Democratic primary (the race for the Democratic nomination). When the election rolled around in November, he easily won that too.

Only thirty-two years old and the youngest governor in the nation, Bill Clinton was nicknamed the boy governor. He and Rodham moved into the enormous Arkansas Governor's Mansion in Little Rock, complete with a cook and other staff members. Rodham continued working at the Rose Law Firm, which made her a partner (part owner) shortly after the election. As a

Hillary Rodham stands beside her husband as he takes the oath of office as governor of Arkansas in 1978.

partner, she earned far more money than her husband did as governor. She was just thirty-two as well. Neither could believe that they had come so far so fast.

ARKANSAS BACKLASH

Many older, more traditional Arkansas citizens did not like the new governor or his wife, however. Although Bill Clinton was an Arkansas native, some people considered him an outsider. He had attended high-tone colleges on the East Coast, and many of his staff members were easterners. He had liberal views on social issues, such as woman's rights. Some people called him a "long-haired hippie."

But critics saved their worst remarks for Hillary Rodham. Rodham had never paid much attention to fashion. Although she dressed in business attire on the job, she felt most comfortable in big sweaters and blue jeans. She wore thick, oversized glasses and refused to wear makeup. She had long, straight hair, which she rarely curled or styled. To many Arkansans, Rodham did not look like a proper state First Lady. They wanted a First Lady who wore a fashionable hairdo, cute outfits, jewelry, and lots of makeup. To make matters worse, Rodham was a Yankee, or northerner—an outsider who did not , many felt, understand or fit into Arkansas's southern culture. She was also an outspoken and ambitious businesswoman. That didn't sit right with some Arkansans either. They thought the governor's wife should be a prim and proper housewife.

While she was working hard as a lawyer and trying to adjust to her new role as First Lady, Rodham became pregnant. On February 17, 1980, she gave birth to a baby girl, Chelsea, named after a Joni Mitchell song, "Chelsea Morning." Chelsea was born a few weeks early, but she was healthy and weighed slightly over six pounds. The Clintons were thrilled with their new baby. However, when newspapers reported that "Governor Bill Clinton and Hillary Rodham had a daughter," many citizens were offended.

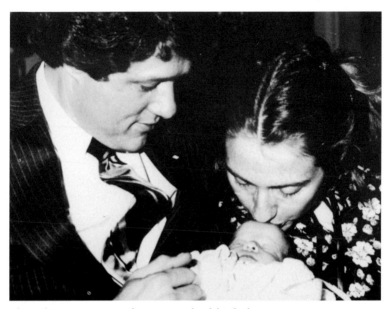

The Clintons pose with one-week-old Chelsea in 1980.

The majority of Arkansans thought the announcement should have read "Governor and Mrs. Bill Clinton."

Bill Clinton made some important strides for Arkansas during his term in office, including—with the help of his wife—reforming the state's health care system. But some voters were still unhappy with his personal and political views. In 1980 Bill Clinton lost his bid for reelection. He was disappointed and depressed.

A Comeback

The family left the Governor's Mansion and bought an old home in Little Rock. With the help of babysitters and nannies for Chelsea, Rodham and Clinton juggled work and parenthood. Bill Clinton took a job with a Little Rock law firm, but he was determined to win back the governor's job.

Rodham wanted to help her husband win any way she could, and she knew she might have to make some compromises to do so. So in early 1982, when Clinton announced that he was again running for governor, Rodham tried to give voters the image they wanted in a First Lady. For starters, she began calling herself Hillary Rodham Clinton. She also livened up her appearance with a new hairstyle with blonde streaks, contact lenses instead of glasses, lipstick and eye shadow, and a fashionable wardrobe.

Together the Clintons began to campaign nonstop. Hillary sat in on planning sessions and supported and encouraged her husband when he grew disheartened or tired. And she did a great job of convincing voters to accept his ideas and plans for the government.

The campaign was a success, and Bill won reelection in late 1982. Right away, he appointed Hillary as chairperson of the state's new Arkansas Education Standards Committee. The committee's job was to set standards for the quality of education throughout the state. Hillary traveled all over Arkansas to hold hearings and meet with groups of parents and teachers. In the end, the committee recommended some important changes, including required tests for teachers to prove their ability to teach.

More popular than he had been during his first term, Bill Clinton won reelection again in 1984 and 1986. Hillary remained involved in state programs. In 1985 she established the Home Instruction Program for Preschool Youth (HIPPY), which taught low-income Arkansas parents how to prepare their children for kindergarten. All the while, she practiced law, raised Chelsea, and continued her work on behalf of children. She served on the board of directors of several educational and social justice organizations, including the Children's Defense Fund. She also performed the jobs expected of a governor's wife, such as hosting teas and attending luncheons.

The family traveled and enjoyed their time together. But Hillary also had some worries. First and foremost, Bill Clinton had a reputation as a womanizer—a man who flirted, chased women, and cheated on his wife. On and off, rumors surfaced that Governor Clinton was having affairs with other women. The rumors hurt Hillary, but Bill assured her that they were untrue.

TAKING THE LEAP

In 1987 Bill Clinton was forty years old. His popularity and successes in Arkansas were well known. Many Democratic leaders began encouraging him to run for president of the United States. He and Hillary discussed the idea carefully, but they decided it was too soon. They knew his opponents would stir up bad press about his rumored affairs with other women.

They thought Chelsea, then aged seven, was too young to be exposed to the difficulties and possible ugliness of such a campaign.

But four years later, after another two terms as governor, Bill Clinton was ready to step up to the next level. By then even more Democrats were encouraging Clinton to run for president. Finally, one morning in August 1991, Hillary woke up and peered into her husband's sleepy face. "You almost have to do it," she said—meaning run for president.

"Do you have any idea what we're getting into?" he asked.

"I know, it'll be tough," she answered.

But they were both ready for the challenge of a lifetime.

Hillary Rodham Clinton campaigns for her husband during the 1992 presidential election.

Chapter **FIVE**

"THE RACE IS ON"

ON OCTOBER 3, 1991, BILL CLINTON STOOD IN front of the Old State House in Little Rock and announced his intention to run for president of the United States. Amid a sea of microphones and TV cameras, he spoke passionately about the problems facing the nation: "Middle-class people are spending more time on the job, less time with their children and bringing home less money to pay more for health care and housing and education," he said. "The poverty rates are up, the streets are meaner and ever more children are growing up in broken families. Our country is headed in the wrong direction, fast." Clinton promised a new vision for the United States. He said that as president, he would bring more job opportunities, a better economy, and better schools and health care services to Americans.

As usual, Hillary stood by his side as he spoke, as did Chelsea. The speech kicked off a whirlwind campaign that lasted more than a year and took the Clintons to every corner of the nation. As in earlier elections, Hillary was an integral part of her husband's campaign team. She took a leave of absence from the Rose Law Firm to work on the campaign full-time. She helped Bill write speeches and took part in planning sessions.

Campaigning in New Hampshire one day, Clinton talked to supporters about his wife's extensive experience working on behalf of children and the poor. He explained that if he were elected, his wife would be an active partner in his new administration. He joked that "Buy one, get one free," should be his new campaign slogan.

Not everyone thought the joke was funny. Just like the voters in Arkansas, Americans in other places had a distinct image of how a national First Lady should act. They thought she should be quiet and ladylike, attending to social matters but in no way involved in running the government. Former president Richard Nixon summed up the feelings of many Americans when he commented about the Clintons, "If the wife comes through as being too strong and too intelligent, it makes the husband look like a wimp."

"STAND BY YOUR MAN"

The Clintons were no strangers to criticism. And after Bill's twelve years as governor, they were no strangers to mean-spirited political campaigns. So they shrugged off the negative comments and continued their campaign travels.

But the attacks got even harsher. Like all political candidates, the Clintons were put under the microscope. The press combed through every detail of their personal lives, hounding their family members for childhood stories and photos and needling their friends for juicy tidbits about them. Not surprisingly, it wasn't long before rumors of Bill's extramarital affairs came to light in the media. According to one gossip magazine, a woman named Gennifer Flowers claimed to have had a twelve-year affair with Bill Clinton. Soon the story was all over television and the newspapers.

The story threatened to overshadow Bill Clinton's message about important issues facing the country. To put the rumors to rest, his campaign team decided that he and Hillary should go on TV's *60 Minutes* news show to set the record straight. The show aired right after the Super Bowl, on January 26, 1992, so a large audience was watching. During the interview, Bill denied having an extramarital affair with Gennifer Flowers. He added that he and Hillary loved each other very much but like all couples had had some difficult moments in their marriage.

Then Hillary added a comment of her own: "You know, I'm not sitting here, some little woman standing by my man like Tammy Wynette. I'm sitting here because I love him and I respect him and I honor

Gennifer Flowers held an interview in New York City in January 1992 to answer questions about her alleged twelve-year affair with Bill Clinton.

what he's been through and what we've been through together. And you know, if that's not enough for people, then heck, don't vote for him."

Hillary was referring to Tammy Wynette's famous country song "Stand by Your Man." The song tells women to stick by their husbands through thick and thin, to love them without question, and to forgive them when they stray. Hillary's reference to the song stirred up more controversy. By belittling the lyrics, some people thought she was attacking traditional marriage and motherhood.

It seemed that Hillary's words were constantly being twisted, and offhand remarks kept coming back to haunt her. Another misunderstanding took place in Chicago in March, when a reporter asked her about charges of questionable dealings between the Rose Law Firm and the Arkansas state government. In explaining the situation, Hillary said: "You know, I suppose I could have stayed home and baked cookies and had teas, but what I decided to do was fulfill my profession, which I entered before my husband was in public life."

Hillary went on to say that she supported whatever a woman chose to do—whether that was working full-time, staying home with her kids, or doing some combination of both. But only the "cookies" comment made the evening news. Again, it seemed like Hillary was putting down homemakers.

To be sure, Hillary Clinton was a proud feminist—someone who believes in complete equality between men and women. Some American voters—especially young women and working women—loved her bold statements, strong opinions, and professional achievements. But other, more traditional voters were put off by a woman who was ambitious and independent.

THE HOME STRETCH

Bill Clinton had his backers and his attackers too. During the primary race, he spoke in favor of abortion rights, gun control, and social programs. His liberal stances angered many conservative Americans.

The press reported that during the Vietnam War, Bill Clinton, like many young men of the era, had tried to avoid military service. Many traditional Americans said he was unpatriotic.

But even with these criticisms, Bill Clinton's popularity soared. In July 1992, at the Democratic National Convention, he officially became his party's candidate for president. He would square off against President George H. W. Bush, the Republican candidate, and H. Ross Perot, an independent (a candidate not affiliated with any party).

Through the rest of the summer and into the fall, Bill and Hillary traveled by bus, together with vice presidential candidate Al Gore and his wife, Tipper. They traveled thousands of miles, making speeches and boosting their support among voters. Hillary and Tipper became close friends during the journey.

Hillary Rodham Clinton and Tipper Gore, right, campaign on behalf of their husbands in 1992.

The Clintons did the best they could to shield their young daughter from the media during the 1992 presidential campaign.

While Bill and Hillary traveled, Chelsea stayed out of the spotlight. Hillary's parents had moved to Little Rock a few years earlier. They, along with Bill's mother and sometimes nannies, took care of Chelsea during the campaign. Chelsea was only twelve years old in 1992. Hillary and Bill tried hard—sometimes unsuccessfully—to shield her from reporters. They also helped her cope with the criticisms of her parents that kept surfacing in the press.

The Clintons returned home to Little Rock on the morning of election day, November 3, 1992. They voted and then rested—but only briefly. Bill and Chelsea went for a jog together during the afternoon, and he later dropped into a neighborhood McDonald's for a soft drink and conversation with other customers. During the long evening, the family gathered with friends at the Arkansas Governor's Mansion and watched the election results on television. Bill Clinton was winning state after state.

Around ten that evening, President Bush conceded defeat. Bill Clinton would be the next president of the United States. Outside the Old Statehouse in Little Rock, crowds began to celebrate. Along with the Gores, the Clintons arrived on stage and waved to thousands of spectators and reporters. Bill gave a

The Gores, left, and the Clintons, right, celebrate their victory in the 1992 bid for the White House.

brief acceptance speech, and then the celebration continued. Bill and Hillary danced together to the old rock tune that had become the campaign's official song, Fleetwood Mac's "Don't Stop (Thinking about Tomorrow)." The long, hard race was over. The next stop was the White House, the president's home in Washington, D.C.

Hillary Rodham Clinton was forty-six years old when she became First Lady of the United States in 1993.

Chapter **SIX**

WOMAN IN THE WEST WING

ON JANUARY 21, 1993, WILLIAM JEFFERSON Clinton was sworn in as the forty-second president of the United States. Of course, the day represented a huge milestone for Bill. But Hillary and Chelsea, too, were faced with big changes. The whole family, along with their cat, Socks, moved to the White House at 1600 Pennsylvania Avenue in Washington, D.C. For Hillary, moving to Washington meant giving up her job at the Rose Law Firm and stepping into the role of First Lady. For Chelsea the move to Washington meant a new school and new friends and living in the bright spotlight as the daughter of the president of the United States.

Because Bill was a longtime governor, the family had been well known in Arkansas. They were used to security guards and swarms of reporters. But as the

First Family, their fame was far greater. Bill, Hillary and Chelsea each had a team of Secret Service agents assigned to protect them around the clock. If Hillary wanted to take a quiet walk or bike ride, not only would several agents have to accompany her, but others would follow behind in a van.

Thirteen-year-old Chelsea enrolled in Sidwell Friends School, a small private school in Washington, D.C. Bill and Hillary had always promoted public education, so the decision to enroll their daughter in a private school caused a stir in the press. But Bill and Hillary were most concerned with shielding Chelsea's privacy. Private schools were off-limits to TV and newspaper reporters, whereas public schools were not. At Sidwell Friends, reporters could not bother Chelsea.

First Lady of Health Care

Bill Clinton had discussed many pressing issues when he ran for president. He often spoke about problems with the nation's health care system. Health insurance was so expensive that millions of people couldn't afford it, he explained. Many people got sick and even died because they couldn't pay to see a doctor. He promised that if he were elected president, he would reform the insurance industry and the health care system in the United States.

Clinton knew the perfect person to handle such an important job—a person with years of experience working on behalf of families, children, working people, and the poor—a person who had successfully reformed the educational system in Arkansas. That person was his wife, Hillary Rodham Clinton. On January 25, less than a week after his inauguration, President Clinton appointed Hillary to head his Task Force on National Health Care Reform.

No one was surprised to learn that Hillary Clinton would devote herself to an important cause. After all, several earlier First Ladies had worked on social issues. Eleanor Roosevelt, the wife of President Franklin D. Roosevelt, had worked tirelessly on behalf of minorities and the poor. President Lyndon Johnson's wife, Lady Bird, had devoted herself to beautifying the nation's highways and cities. Nancy Reagan, the wife of President Ronald Reagan, had spoken out against illegal drug use. But what was surprising was the nature of Hillary Clinton's assignment. No other First Lady had held an official job making government policy.

In addition to heading the health care task force (she was not paid for the job), Hillary had a number of other jobs as First Lady. In keeping with tradition, she was the official White House hostess, in charge of overseeing dinners and receptions. She also had to make speeches, attend conferences, welcome foreign leaders, and visit foreign countries. She had a staff of twenty, including speechwriters, research assistants, travel directors, social directors, and secretaries.

Hillary set up her office in the West Wing of the White House. This was another break with tradition. First Ladies had always made their offices in the East Wing, not the West Wing, where the president and his senior advisers worked. But Hillary wanted her staff to be integrated with the rest of the White House staff. Their work on health care and other issues was just as important as everyone else's, she believed.

ROUGH WATERS

After all the earlier criticism, it wasn't surprising that many people also criticized Hillary for leading the task force on health care. They accused her of trying to grab too much power. Once when she was speaking in Lincoln, Nebraska, in April 1993, a woman held up a sign reading, "Hillary, Who Elected You President?" Other people posted signs that said "Impeach Hillary," implying that she, not her husband, was running the country. People also made jokes about "President Clinton and her husband, Bill."

Hillary was tough. She took the criticism in stride and continued her work on health care and other issues. But on both a personal and a professional level, the family faced one difficulty after another. First, on March 19, 1993, Hillary's father suffered a massive stroke. The family flew to Little Rock to be by his bedside. He died less than three weeks later.

After a period of mourning, Bill and Hillary got back to work. But it seemed like bad news just kept coming. In May financial auditors found evidence of mismanagement in the White House Travel Office. It was a small matter, but critics of the Clintons blew it out of proportion, calling it Travelgate—a nickname that echoed the Watergate scandal of twenty years before.

A few months later, Deputy White House Counsel Vince Foster, an old friend of Hillary's from the Rose Law Firm, was found dead in a park outside Washington, D.C. He appeared to have committed suicide. But rumors swirled that his death was a murder and was somehow related to Travelgate—or perhaps to more sinister dealings within the Clinton administration.

One of the few bright spots came in September and October, when Hillary and Bill introduced their health care reform legislation (a group of laws) to Congress. Along with other changes, the proposed plan included affordable health insurance for every American. Hillary was just the third First Lady to ever testify before Congress and the first to introduce major legislation. Those who heard her speak were impressed by her command of the complex health care issue. Both Democrats and Republicans applauded her testimony and praised her recommendations for change. The lawmaking process is often slow, and the proposed reforms still had a long way to go before they would become law, but both Hillary and Bill were encouraged by the response.

December 1993 was another dark period. It began when federal investigators accused the Whitewater

Development Company, a corporation in Arkansas, of financial wrongdoing. The Clintons had been partners in the corporation when they lived in Arkansas. They denied they had ever acted illegally, but to clear the air, President Clinton promised to have the matter investigated.

About the same time the Whitewater charges hit the papers, more accusations came to light about Bill Clinton's womanizing during his days as Arkansas governor. The new stories, nicknamed Troopergate because they originated with Arkansas state troopers, were untrue. Bill and Hillary suspected that their political enemies had paid the troopers to make the accusations.

The next year, 1994, was hardly any better. In January Bill Clinton's mother, Virginia Kelley, died of breast cancer. Then Paula Jones, a former Arkansas state employee, accused Bill Clinton of sexual harassment (unwelcome sexual advances). Then an independent counsel (lawyer), appointed by federal judges, began investigating the Whitewater affair.

Finally, perhaps most disappointing of all for Hillary, her health care plan "died" in Congress (was dropped from consideration) without ever coming to a vote. Millions of Americans supported her ideas for affordable health care. But insurance companies, drug companies, and other powerful groups had lobbied hard to discredit the plan, worried that it would cut into their profits.

Rumors of affairs continued to plague Clinton during his years as president. Paula Jones, right, sued him for sexual harassment in 1994.

By late 1994, Bill Clinton was finishing his second year as president. It seemed as if his Republican opponents had spent the previous two or three years doing nothing but attacking his wife, searching for scandals in his personal and business affairs, criticizing his policies, and investigating him. With all the negative press, voters seemed wary of Bill Clinton's Democratic administration. They expressed their displeasure by voting in a majority of Republican congresspeople and senators at the midterm elections in November.

REBOUND

Was Bill Clinton doing a bad job as president? With all the scandals and accusations, it might seem so.

THE ISSUES AND THE PARTIES

Throughout much of the twentieth century and into the twenty-first century, Democrats and Republicans have tended to take opposing views on many issues. Democrats tend to view government as a tool for helping people improve their lives. They generally support the interests of poor and working people over the interests of big business, a view sometimes called liberal or left wing. Republicans, sometimes called conservative or right wing, usually prefer that government not try to solve social problems. They support policies that allow businesses to operate freely, without many government controls.

Labels such as *liberal* and *conservative* can be misleading and inaccurate, however. Many people have conservative views on some issues and liberal views on others. Many wealthy business people support the Democrats, traditionally the party of poor people, and many working-class people support the Republicans, traditionally the party of the rich.

Despite the complexities, many issues do tend to break down along party lines. Here are some major issues that faced the United States during the Clinton administration (and other administrations) and how the two major parties viewed them:

Abortion

- Many Republicans oppose abortion, which they view as the murder of an unborn child.

- Many Democrats support a woman's right to choose an abortion. They believe women, with the advice of their doctors, should make their own decisions about whether or not to give birth.

Environmental Protection

- Many Republicans oppose environmental laws that cost businesses a lot of money. For instance, they oppose laws that require businesses to install expensive equipment to clean smokestacks and cut down on air pollution.

- Many Democrats favor strong environmental protection laws, even if the laws cost businesses a lot of money.

Gun Control

- Many Republicans oppose gun control laws because the Second Amendment of the U.S. Constitution guarantees citizens the right to bear arms. They also argue that laws do not keep criminals from using guns.

- Many Democrats favor gun control laws as a way to reduce murder and other violent crimes.

Military Spending

- Many Republicans favored a strong military and support spending large amounts of money on weapons, soldiers, and other defense needs.

- Many Democrats think that high defense spending takes money away from other important government programs.

Social Programs

- Many Republicans oppose government spending on social programs. They argue that poor people should work hard to improve their own lives, without government help.

- Many Democrats think the government should help improve the lives of the poor, minorities, women, and children by spending money on social programs.

Taxes

- Many Republicans feel that taxes (money citizens pay to the government) should be kept low. They argue that the economy will improve if people keep more of their earnings and pay less in taxes.

- Many Democrats feel that high taxes are necessary to fund government programs. They feel that the wealthiest Americans have a responsibility to pay the most taxes.

But in fact the opposite was true. Under Bill Clinton's watch, the U.S. economy was booming and unemployment was falling. The national debt—the vast sums of money the United States owed to other nations—was falling too. Inflation (rising prices) was low. Although he often had to fight with Republicans in Congress, especially Georgia congressman Newt Gingrich, Clinton was able to pass a number of important laws, such as gun control bills, environmental protection laws, and a minimum wage increase.

As for Hillary, she began to keep a lower profile after the defeat of her health care plan. She no longer tried to promote major policy reforms. Instead, she traveled and met with foreign leaders, attended conferences, wrote articles, and made speeches. She continued to work on the issues that had always interested her: children's rights, women's rights, education, and improving life for the poor.

First Lady Eleanor Roosevelt had for many years written a newspaper column called "My Day." Hillary revered Roosevelt. Modeling herself on her hero, she started writing her own weekly newspaper column called "Talking It Over." In this column, she discussed issues of concern to her, such as family life, education, and health care.

Of course, Hillary still had a job as a mother. Chelsea, then in high school, was getting ready to choose a college. She needed her mother's guidance and support.

HILLARY'S HERO

hen Hillary Rodham Clinton moved into the White House, she followed in the footsteps of some famous First Ladies. Some of them had star power. President John F. Kennedy's wife, Jacqueline, for instance, was a breathtaking socialite who set trends with her hairstyles, clothing, and cultural activities. Nancy Reagan was a former actress who loved to dress in fancy gowns and throw elaborate formal parties at the White House.

But Hillary Clinton looked for her role model to a more humble, down-to-earth First Lady, Eleanor Roosevelt. Like Hillary Clinton, Eleanor Roosevelt cared deeply about the plight of the nation's poor and minority groups. During her husband's four terms in office (1933–1945), she used her position as First Lady to speak out about causes she believed in. She gave speeches and wrote magazine and newspaper articles. After her husband's death, Roosevelt worked with the United Nations as a champion for human rights. Like Hillary Clinton, she was often criticized for "meddling" in government affairs.

As First Lady, Hillary Clinton often spoke about her admiration for Eleanor Roosevelt. "I am a die-hard Eleanor Roosevelt fan," she said at the dedication of the Eleanor Roosevelt College, part of the University of California-San Diego, in 1995. "I have read her autobiography, her newspaper columns, and many books about her and President Roosevelt."

Clinton even admitted to having imaginary conversations with Roosevelt, asking for her advice on a range of topics and problems. Whenever criticism of her or the president got particularly harsh, Hillary would "ask" Eleanor Roosevelt for her opinion. "I try to figure out what she would do in my shoes," Hillary once said. "She usually responds by telling me to buck up or at least to grow skin as thick as a rhinoceros."[31]

In late 1994, Hillary began a new project. She decided to write a book about raising children in modern society. The book took its inspiration from an African saying, "It takes a village to raise a child." Hillary explained, "I chose that old African proverb [saying] to title this book because it offers a timeless reminder that children will thrive only if their families thrive and if the whole of society cares enough to provide for them."

When she wasn't traveling or appearing at special events, Hillary sat down to work on the book. She recorded her thoughts on children's health, education, and nutrition, and keeping children safe in a fast-paced, often troubled society. She wrote about ways that government could help children and parents, such as by funding child care programs and family leave (time off from work) for new parents. She completed the manuscript in late 1995, and the finished product, *It Takes a Village and Other Lessons Children Teach Us,* appeared on bookstore shelves in early 1996. Then Hillary set out across the country on a book-signing tour. People were eager to meet with her and buy her book. *It Takes a Village* became an immediate best-seller.

Though still haunted by scandals and investigations, Bill Clinton remained popular with a majority of the American people. In the Gallup organization's yearly poll, he had been named the Most Admired Man in the United States each year since taking office. (Hillary also won top honors as the Most Admired

Woman each year.) When he ran for president in 1996 against Republican Bob Dole, he again won by a wide margin. With the troubles of the first term behind them, Bill and Hillary were excited to continue their hard work on behalf of the American people.

Hillary and Chelsea in South Africa in 1997

Chapter SEVEN

"THIS VAST RIGHT-WING CONSPIRACY"

THE DAWN OF BILL CLINTON'S SECOND TERM IN office, winter 1997, was a positive time for the Clinton family. Chelsea was a senior in high school. She planned to attend Stanford University in California in the fall. In March 1997, Hillary and Chelsea took a trip to Africa, visiting several countries. During the trip, they came face-to-face with despair—such as the AIDS epidemic (widespread outbreak) that was devastating many African nations. And they came face-to-face with hope—such as the new democratic government in South Africa, where apartheid (the forced separation of blacks and whites) had recently ended.

As for Bill, he was confident that his legal troubles were just about over. The Whitewater investigation, by

Madeleine Albright, right, became the highest-ranking woman in the history of the U.S. government when she became secretary of state in 1997.

then led by attorney Kenneth Starr, appeared to be winding down. Although several of the Clintons' former business partners had been charged with crimes, the Clintons had not been charged. It also appeared that Paula Jones would drop her lawsuit against Bill. He could finally get on with the business of running the country. As part of his new administration, he appointed Madeleine Albright as secretary of state. She was the first woman ever to hold this position, one of the most important posts in the U.S. government.

HOUSEHOLD TRANSITIONS

In the spring of 1997, Chelsea Clinton graduated from Sidwell Friends School. The commencement speaker at her graduation ceremony was none other than the president of the United States—Bill Clinton. Later in the summer, the family vacationed on Martha's Vineyard in Massachusetts.

When September arrived, both Bill and Hillary were glum. It was time for Chelsea to start college at Stanford. When Hillary had first learned that Chelsea wanted to go to Stanford, just south of San Francisco in California, she protested, "What! Stanford is too far away! You can't go that far away. That's all the way over on the West Coast—three time zones away." But by moving day, Hillary had calmed down. She was thrilled to see her daughter setting out on her own path. Bill and Hillary helped Chelsea settle in at her college dormitory and met some of her new college classmates.

When Bill and Hillary returned home, however, they were filled with loneliness. The solution, they decided, was to get a dog. Hillary located a three-month-old chocolate Labrador and presented him to Bill as a Christmas present. They decided to name him Buddy, after Bill's favorite uncle, who had recently died. The new puppy brightened Bill and Hillary's spirits while they missed Chelsea. But one member of the household didn't like Buddy. Socks, the family cat, hissed whenever Buddy approached and once even swiped him on the nose.

OLD AND NEW DEMONS

In January 1998, all Bill Clinton's legal troubles seemed to collapse into one another. That month Ken

Starr, head of the Whitewater investigation team, expanded his investigation. In a turn of events that shocked and confused the public, Starr's team charged that during the Paula Jones sexual harassment case, Clinton had lied about a sexual affair with a young White House intern, Monica Lewinsky, and had asked Lewinsky to lie about the affair as well. Starr's legal team said that lying and encouraging Lewinsky to lie were impeachable offenses—Clinton could be removed from office if he were found guilty.

Hillary Clinton had heard it all before. She'd heard all the gossip about her husband's extramarital affairs. She'd heard all the false charges of Troopergate. The

Monica Lewinksy is escorted into a Los Angeles courtroom during the investigation of her affair with Bill Clinton.

Lewinsky story, she assumed, was just another lie cooked up by Bill Clinton's Republican opponents to discredit him. What's more, Bill had told her all about the charges and assured her they were untrue. He did know the young intern, he explained, but he certainly hadn't had an affair with her.

So when TV host Matt Lauer asked Hillary about the Lewinsky matter on the *Today* show one morning, Hillary was quick to give her take on the situation. First, she explained that, after five years as First Lady, she was quite used to unseemly rumors and the excitement that followed. "We're right in the middle of a rather vigorous feeding frenzy [media uproar] right now," she started, "and people are saying all kinds of things and putting out rumor[s]. . . . And I have learned over the last many years being involved in politics, and especially since my husband first started running for President, that the best thing to do in these cases is just to be patient, take a deep breath and the truth will come out."

Then she went on to describe what she felt was the real source of the attacks against her husband. She said, "The great story here for anybody willing to find it and write about it and explain it is this vast right-wing conspiracy that has been conspiring against my husband since the day he announced for president."

A vast right-wing conspiracy? Had the right wing—that is, extreme conservatives—made up the Lewinsky story to disgrace Bill Clinton and then to bring impeachment charges against him? Hillary Clinton thought so.

WORLD FAMOUS

s First Lady, Hillary Clinton was one of the most famous women on the planet. She was recognized everywhere she went, and during her eight years as First Lady, she went nearly everywhere on earth. Many people were eager to meet her and hear her speak, and she welcomed the opportunity to discuss causes she believed in, especially women's rights. In 1995 she spoke at the United Nations' Fourth World Conference on Women in Beijing, China. Also in 1995, she and Chelsea traveled to India, Pakistan, Nepal, Sri Lanka, and Bangladesh, focusing their attention on improving women's rights in those countries.

During her travels, Hillary met people who were just as famous as she was. She met prime ministers, presidents, kings, and queens. She met Princess Diana, *right*, the ex-wife of Britain's Prince Charles. She met Mother Teresa, a nun known worldwide for her tireless work on behalf of India's poorest people. Hillary became good friends with former First Lady Jackie Kennedy Onassis, who gave her advice on raising a daughter in the White House. She got to know entertainers and sports stars, too, including singers Aretha Franklin, Elton John, and Stevie Wonder; talk show host David Letterman; and basketball star Scottie Pippen.

She later described this conspiracy as "an interlocking network of groups and individuals who want to turn the clock back on many of the advances our country has made, from civil rights and women's rights to consumer and environmental regulation, and they use all the tools at their disposal—money, power, influence, media and politics—to achieve their ends. In recent years, they have also mastered the politics of personal destruction."

Many people agreed with Hillary. On February 9, *Newsweek* magazine published a chart outlining the financial and organizational links between conservative politicians, groups, and others; the various scandals associated with Clinton's presidency; and the Starr investigation. Soon after, David Brock, author of a 1994 magazine article that had stirred up the Troopergate scandal, admitted that he had been paid to write false accusations by groups determined to destroy Bill Clinton's presidency. Brock apologized to the president for his part in the incident.

CONFESSION

Despite this newest controversy, Bill Clinton continued to push forward with his agenda on national and international issues. In April he helped finalize a groundbreaking peace treaty in Northern Ireland, a region that had been torn apart by terrorism and religious conflict for centuries. Hillary immersed herself in her own work, such as the Save America's Treasures program, a project to protect and restore revered artifacts of U.S. history, such as the flag that inspired the writing of the "The Star-Spangled Banner," the U.S. national anthem.

Then, on the morning of August 15, Bill woke Hillary with some shocking news. Pacing back and forth in their bedroom, he admitted that the Monica Lewinsky rumors were true. He had had a brief affair with the young woman, he confessed. Hillary was angry and heartbroken. Two days after confessing to his wife, Bill addressed the nation on television and made the same confession. In his speech, he apologized for his behavior but defended his right to privacy.

Clinton poses for the media in the White House Map Room minutes before his televised address admitting his affair with Monica Lewinsky.

As Hillary struggled to come to terms with her husband's betrayal, the media uproar got even louder. Republicans called for Bill Clinton's impeachment. Some called for his resignation. Most Democrats felt that Clinton should be reprimanded (denounced) for his affair with Lewinsky but that impeachment was not fitting. He had made a terrible mistake, true, but his private actions certainly hadn't harmed the government or the American people. Historians and constitutional scholars agreed that Bill Clinton's offenses were not grounds for impeachment.

Hillary remained hurt and angry at her husband, but she also argued that his mistakes were a private matter and certainly not punishable by impeachment. And even though her husband had lied to her, she stood by her claim that a right-wing network was trying to destroy his presidency.

The American public seemed to be mostly on President Clinton's side. Although few could excuse his private behavior, about 60 percent of Americans polled said that Clinton should not be impeached for his actions, nor did they think he should resign. Interestingly, Hillary Clinton's approval ratings (a measure of the public's support for her) improved during this period. It appeared that people around the country sympathized with her personal problems.

However, many people, especially women, wondered how she could stay with a cheating husband. In fact, Hillary did consider leaving Bill, but she took her time deciding. She and Bill began marital counseling after he came clean about the Lewinsky affair. Hillary also spoke privately with Donald Jones, her youth minister from her teenage years in Illinois who had become a lifelong friend. After long weeks of soul-searching, Hillary decided to stick with her marriage to Bill and try to improve their relationship.

Meanwhile, the impeachment process moved forward. On September 9, Kenneth Starr delivered a 445-page report to Congress describing Bill Clinton's affair with Monica Lewinsky. The original cause of the investigation, Whitewater, was barely mentioned in the report. In December the U.S. House of Representatives impeached the president on two charges: perjury (lying under oath) and obstruction of justice

Kenneth Starr holds a copy of his report during an impeachment hearing in November 1998.

(blocking the progress of a legal case). Finding the president quilty of these charges and removing him from office would require a two-thirds vote of the Senate.

The highly publicized impeachment trial started on January 7, 1999, and lasted five weeks. In February the Senate found Clinton not guilty, and he served out his term as president. He did his usual good work, for example trying to negotiate a peace agreement between Israeli prime minister Ehud Barak and Palestinian leader Yasser Arafat. But Clinton's reputation was stained, and his marriage was strained. His two terms had been scarred by scandal and political mudslinging. In 2000, when Vice President Al Gore ran for president, Gore deliberately distanced himself from his former running mate.

Hillary Rodham Clinton shakes Congressman Rick Lazio's hand before their second debate during her 2000 run for the U.S. Senate.

Chapter **EIGHT**

SENATOR CLINTON

THE 2000 PRESIDENTIAL RACE FEATURED DEMOCRAT Al Gore, Bill Clinton's vice president, against Republican George W. Bush, son of the first President George Bush. The race was expected to be close. Americans and the media followed the conventions, campaign speeches, political advertisements, and candidate debates with interest.

But another intriguing campaign was under way that year: Hillary Clinton's run for Senate in New York. After moving to New York to establish residency and then winning her party's nomination in mid-May, Clinton hit the campaign trail. Chelsea took time off from school to help her mother campaign. Clinton's original opponent, Mayor Rudolph Giuliani, had dropped out of the race due to health concerns. Her new opponent was Republican congressman Rick Lazio.

Lazio tried some negative campaigning. He tried to paint Clinton as a "pushy" feminist. He called her a carpetbagger because she had moved to New York only a month before the race began. He tried to convince New York's Jewish voters that she didn't support the Jewish state of Israel. He even made an outrageous accusation that she had links to a Middle Eastern terrorist organization.

But Clinton never attacked Lazio in return. She stuck to issues that New York voters cared about: jobs, health care, opportunities for minorities, and the environment. She spent a lot of time in rural upstate New York, learning about the issues that troubled farmers and small-town citizens there. She spent time in Manhattan, listening to the concerns of city dwellers. She attended community events and visited college campuses. Voters everywhere lined up to meet her, and they liked what they heard and saw. And rather than finding her "pushy," many voters—especially women—loved her strength and her support for family, children, and health care issues such as breast cancer research.

One thing voters didn't like was Clinton's donning of a New York Yankees baseball cap on the campaign trail. Since she had only recently moved to New York (and had always rooted for the Chicago Cubs in the past), they thought that acting like a Yankees fan was

Clinton chats with New York Yankees owner George Steinbrenner. Some New Yorkers were offended when Clinton, a lifelong Cubs fan, put on a Yankees cap.

insincere. Voters and newspaper reporters didn't hesitate to criticize her for it.

Clinton took a lead over Lazio in the polls. When election day came, she beat out Lazio 55 percent to 43 percent, becoming the only First Lady ever to win an elected public office. The family was joyful, but it was hard to be completely upbeat. The presidential race had a rocky ending. After a too-close-to-call vote in Florida and a subsequent dispute over recounting the ballots there, the U.S. Supreme Court named George W. Bush the winner of the 2000 presidential

Clinton celebrates her Senate win with Senator Daniel Moynihan. Standing behind her are Chelsea and Bill Clinton.

election. Despite Hillary Clinton's victory, it was a dark time for the Democratic Party.

AT WORK IN WASHINGTON

Hillary Clinton was sworn in as a member of the U.S. Senate on January 3, 2001. For twenty-five years, she had played a supporting role in her husband's political career. Finally, it was her turn to take the lead.

Along with a staff of twenty-seven, she settled into an office on the fourth floor of the Russell Senate Office Building in Washington, D.C. She and Bill also bought and renovated a six-bedroom, $2.9 million house in an exclusive Washington, D.C., neighborhood. This would be Hillary's home when she worked in the nation's capital. Her mother, Dorothy Rodham, would live there too. When her schedule allowed, Hillary would return to her house in Chappaqua, New York.

During the early months of 2001, Hillary Clinton watched and learned. As a brand-new elected official and one of one hundred senators, she didn't have much clout, or influence, in the Senate. And some people predicted that Republican senators who hadn't liked her husband wouldn't like her either. But she remained enthusiastic. "I have worked with a number of Republican [Senate] members in the past," she said. "I'm looking forward to working with them on a bipartisan [two parties working together] basis on issues that affect their states, as well as New York, and of course our entire country."

Clinton began her work in the Senate by introducing bills that would benefit New Yorkers, especially those in rural areas. The first bill she presented helped rural communities get broadband (high-speed) communications access. Another bill involved the building of a new $100 million border-crossing station between upstate New York and Canada.

Clinton showed herself to be focused and a fast learner. She impressed other senators with her command of the issues that came to the Senate for consideration. Even Republicans praised her. Republican senator Trent Lott, who had frequently fought with

President Clinton and made negative remarks about Hillary during her Senate campaign, was impressed by the new senator from New York. He saw her as a hard worker who didn't try to use her fame as a former First Lady to her advantage. "I think she's doing fine," he said. "I think she's trying to dig in and do her homework, trying to lower her profile a little bit." Clinton also teamed up with several Republican senators to sponsor legislation in areas ranging from military spending to nursing.

THE NEW WORLD AT WAR

September 11, 2001 (9/11), was a dark day for the nation and especially for New York City. On that day, terrorists hijacked four airplanes and crashed two of them into the World Trade Center towers in New York City and another into the Pentagon, the U.S. military headquarters near Washington, D.C. A fourth plane, likely bound for the U.S. Capitol, crashed in the Pennsylvania countryside after passengers struggled with the hijackers. Altogether, about three thousand people were killed in the attacks.

In New York City, the two World Trade Center towers burned and then collapsed. The damage was massive. Ground Zero—the site of the collapsed towers—looked like a war zone. Along with fellow New York senator Charles Schumer, Clinton was at the forefront of helping the city recover. She and Schumer secured $21.4 billion in federal funding to help New Yorkers clean up and rebuild at Ground Zero. She also provided much-needed emotional support to New Yorkers, especially those who had lost family members in the attack.

With the September 11 attacks, the United States found itself at war. First, the United States invaded Afghanistan, whose government had provided safe haven for the 9/11 terrorists. Next, in early 2003, the United States invaded Iraq, in part because President Bush said he believed that Iraq was stockpiling weapons of mass destruction (nuclear, biological, and chemical weapons).

Senator Clinton voted in favor of the Iraq invasion. But once U.S. troops had occupied Iraq, she criticized the way the administration was carrying out the war. She saw that President Bush was pumping billions and billions of dollars into the war in Iraq while at the same time cutting programs such as education and social services at home. In addition, soon after the war began, it became clear that Iraq had no weapons of mass destruction—Bush's original argument for invading Iraq had been based on faulty information. Along with other Democrats in Congress, Clinton voiced her opposition to the president's policies in Iraq.

LOOKING BACK AND FORWARD

While Senator Clinton was helping the nation through the difficult new "war on terrorism," she also took time to reflect on the past. On nights and weekends, she completed a 534-page autobiography called *Living History*. The book examines her life to the year 2001, from her childhood in Illinois through the Clinton presidency to her run for Senate. Creating the book was a massive project that required the help of ghostwriters—professional authors who did much of the writing based on Hillary's notes and recollections.

Released in June 2003, the book sold more than 1 million copies in the first month after publication. It was translated into thirty-five languages and distributed around the world. In the summer of 2003,

The cover of Clinton's 2003 autobiography

Hillary embarked on a book-signing tour, autograph-
ing an estimated forty-five thousand copies of *Living
History* for eager admirers. Hillary Clinton was more
popular than ever. In both 2002 and 2003, she was
again named the Most Admired Woman in the United
States in the Gallup Poll.

After the book tour, back at work in the Senate,
Hillary joined the Senate Armed Services Committee
(she already sat on the Environment and Public
Works Committee and the Health, Education, Labor,
and Pensions Committee). The Armed Services Committee is the group of senators who study bills related
to military and defense issues. Clinton wanted to serve
on the committee because she thought the nation was
spending too much money on war and too little on
other important projects. She explained:

> I concluded that the war on terrorism is a long-
> term challenge, and that it will be important to
> understand what our military response will be
> and to satisfy myself we're as well defended as we
> need to be. It's also very clear that [the Bush]
> Administration has a strategy to starve the federal
> budget of everything but defense. I think that's a
> mistake to turn our backs on so many of our
> important domestic and international priori-
> ties . . . I wanted to have some understanding and
> influence over how that money [the federal bud-
> get] was going to be spent.

LIFE AFTER THE PRESIDENCY

Bill Clinton has stayed busy since his job as president ended. He heads the William J. Clinton Presidential Foundation, based in Little Rock. The organization is dedicated to five goals:

- The battle against HIV/AIDS
- Racial, ethnic, and religious harmony
- Citizen service in government and the community
- The economic empowerment of poor people
- Leadership development

The foundation has several branches, including the new William J. Clinton Presidential Library and Museum in Little Rock and the Clinton School of Public Service at the University of Arkansas. In addition to his offices in Little Rock, Bill Clinton has an office in the Harlem neighborhood of New York City. He frequently resides with Hillary in Washington, D.C., and at their home in Chappaqua, New York.

In June 2004, Bill Clinton published his own autobiography, *My Life*, which runs more than one thousand pages. In this book, Clinton describes his private and public life, including his childhood, education, family, political career, and the controversies of his presidency. To promote the book, Clinton gave interviews to many TV talk shows. Later, in the summer and fall of 2004, Clinton spoke at the Democratic National Convention in Boston and helped campaign for John F. Kerry, the 2004 Democratic presidential nominee.

During the Thanksgiving holiday in 2003, Clinton visited U.S. troops in Afghanistan and Iraq. She wanted to see firsthand what the soldiers fighting in the Middle East were going through. She paid special attention to troops who hailed from New York. Back at home, she devoted much of her work on the Armed Services Committee to fighting for benefits and health care for military veterans.

In early 2004, Clinton became chairman of the Senate's Democratic Steering Committee—an association of Democrats in the Senate. She also helped create the Center for American Progress, a liberal think tank (research organization).

Clinton visits with U.S. soldiers at Bagram Air Base near Kabul, Afghanistan, in November 2003.

THE FIRST DAUGHTER

s a small child, Chelsea Clinton lived in the Arkansas Governor's Mansion, a grand house in Little Rock. The Clintons tried to give Chelsea a normal childhood. She attended public school in Little Rock, where she earned high grades. One of her favorite hobbies was ballet dancing. Along with her parents, she loved to attend the Arkansas Ballet performance of *The Nutcracker* every year at Christmastime and an annual Renaissance fair at New Year's. Both of Chelsea's parents had busy schedules, so babysitters and her grandparents often cared for her, especially during Bill's first presidential campaign.

Chelsea was twelve when her father became president. At first, her parents shielded her from the media, forbidding reporters to interview her and limiting photographers' access to her. But even though Chelsea had protection from the media, she still didn't have privacy. When she went out with friends, Secret Service agents had to tag along to make sure no one tried to harm her.

When Chelsea turned fifteen, her parents allowed the media more access to her. In April 1995, she and her mother toured India and four nearby nations. The next year, the two traveled through southern Europe. The press followed them closely and photographed them on both trips. For the first time, Chelsea spoke to the news media, offering her impressions of the countries she visited.

Chelsea enrolled in Stanford University in the fall of 1997. There, she majored in history. For her senior thesis, she wrote a 167-page paper on the peace process in Northern Ireland, negotiations in which her father played a key role.

After graduating from Stanford, she entered a master's program in international relations at Oxford University in Great Britain (her father had studied there too). In Great Britain, Chelsea began to date Ian Klaus, *above, with Chelsea,* a Rhodes Scholar from California. She also made friends with celebrities such as Madonna and Gwyneth Paltrow.

In the spring of 2004, Chelsea took a job with the New York office of McKinsey and Company, a worldwide consulting firm. Her position is business analyst, with a specialty in the health care sector. In this role, she consults with companies and helps them improve their business operations.

Shortly afterward, Hillary Clinton received a strange honor. In its March issue, *Men's Journal* magazine named her number twenty-five on its list of "The 25 Toughest Guys in America." Others on the list included Green Bay Packers quarterback Brett Favre and Secretary of Defense Donald Rumsfeld. *Men's Journal* had never put a woman on its "tough guy" list before. Senior editor Tom Foster explained the choice. "I think just looking at what she's been through and what she represents, that sort of stood for itself," he said. And he concluded, "Would you mess with her?"

Clinton and her husband share a kiss at the 2004 dedication of the Clinton presidential library in Little Rock, Arkansas.

What is next for Hillary Clinton? Her senate term ends in 2007. The next logical step, many think, is a campaign for president of the United States. If elected, Clinton would break new ground as the first woman president in the history of the United States. Would she consider running? She's been asked many times, and she's even hinted that she might run. But for the time being, her job is in the Senate, she insists. What do political observers say when asked about the prospects for another Clinton in the White House? "Don't count her out," is the most common answer.

SOURCES

1 Hillary Rodham Clinton, *Living History* (New York: Simon and Schuster, 2003), 498.
2 Ibid., 502.
3 Ibid., 9.
4 Gail Sheehy, *Hillary's Choice* (New York: Random House, 1999), 24.
5 Norman King, *A Woman in the White House: The Remarkable Story of Hillary Rodham Clinton* (New York: Birch Lane Press, 1996), 5.
6 Sheehy, *Hillary's Choice*, 24.
7 King, *A Woman in the White House*, 5.
8 Joyce Milton, *The First Partner: Hillary Rodham Clinton* (New York: William Morrow and Company, Inc., 1999), 14.
9 Ibid., 13.
10 King, *A Woman in the White House*, 10.
11 Clinton, *Living History*, 24.
12 Sheehy, *Hillary's Choice*, 39.
13 Milton, *The First Partner*, 24.
14 Clinton, *Living History*, 37.
15 Ibid., 38.
16 Sheehy, *Hillary's Choice*, 58–59.
17 Clinton, *Living History*, 52.
18 Sheehy, *Hillary's Choice*, 75.
19 Ibid., 82.
20 Clinton, *Living History*, 69.
21 Ibid., 74.
22 King, *A Woman in the White House*, 60.
23 Ibid., 78.
24 Sheehy, *Hillary's Choice*, 196.
25 Clinton, *Living History*, 102.
26 Ibid., 106.
27 Claire G. Osborne, ed., *The Unique Voice of Hillary Rodham Clinton: A Portrait in Her Own Words* (New York: Avon Books, 1997), 47.
28 Clinton, *Living History*, 109.

29 Hillary Rodham Clinton, *It Takes a Village and Other Lessons Children Teach Us* (New York: Simon and Schuster, 1996), 12.
30 Osborne, *The Unique Voice,* 108.
31 Ibid., 109.
32 Clinton, *Living History,* 341.
33 Ibid., 445.
34 Ibid., 446.
35 Elizabeth Kolbert, "The Student," *New Yorker,* October 13, 2003, 65.
36 Ibid.
37 Ibid., 64.
38 "U.S. Men's Magazine Names Hillary Clinton One of 25 'Toughest Guys.'" *Hillary Clinton Forum.* February 20, 2004, http://www.hillary.org (February 21, 2004).

SELECTED BIBLIOGRAPHY

"About Senator Hillary Rodham Clinton," *Senator Hillary Rodham Clinton, 2004.* http://clinton.senate.gov/about_hrc.html (August 9, 2004).

Clinton, Bill. *My Life.* New York: Knopf, 2004.

Clinton, Hillary Rodham. *It Takes a Village and Other Lessons Children Teach Us.* New York: Simon and Schuster, 1996.

———. *Living History.* New York: Simon and Schuster, 2003.

King, Norman. *A Woman in the White House: The Remarkable Story of Hillary Rodham Clinton.* New York: Birch Lane Press, 1996.

Milton, Joyce. *The First Partner: Hillary Rodham Clinton.* New York: William Morrow and Company, Inc., 1999.

Osborne, Claire G., ed. *The Unique Voice of Hillary Rodham Clinton: A Portrait in Her Own Words.* New York: Avon Books, 1997.

Sheehy, Gail. *Hillary's Choice.* New York: Random House, 1999.

FURTHER READING
AND WEBSITES

BOOKS

Benson, Michael. *Bill Clinton.* Minneapolis: Lerner Publications Company, 2004.

Clinton, Hillary Rodham. *Dear Socks, Dear Buddy: Kids' Letters to the First Pets.* New York: Simon and Schuster, 1998.

Freedman, Russell. *Eleanor Roosevelt: A Life of Discovery.* New York: Houghton Mifflin Company, 1997.

Galt, Margot Fortunato. *Stop This War: American Protest of the Conflict in Vietnam.* Minneapolis: Lerner Publications Company, 2000.

Márquez, Herón. *Richard M. Nixon.* Minneapolis: Lerner Publications Company, 2003.

Ryan, Bernard, Jr. *Hillary Rodham Clinton: First Lady and Senator.* New York: Facts on File, 2004.

WEBSITES

"First Ladies' Gallery." *The White House.*
http://www.whitehouse.gov/history/firstladies/
This site offers biographies of every First Lady in U.S. history. Visitors can read about Hillary Clinton, her hero Eleanor Roosevelt, and all the other First Ladies.

Friends of Hillary.
http://www.friendsofhillary.com
This site is devoted to Hillary Clinton and her Senate career. It includes news about her recent work in the Senate, photos, and biographical information. Visitors to the site can also join groups of supporters such as the Hillraisers, Hill's Angels, and Young Voters for Hillary Rodham Clinton.

INDEX

OTHER TITLES FROM LERNER AND A&E®:

Ariel Sharon
Arnold Schwarzenegger
Arthur Ashe
The Beatles
Benjamin Franklin
Bill Gates
Bruce Lee
Carl Sagan
Chief Crazy Horse
Christopher Reeve
Colin Powell
Daring Pirate Women
Edgar Allan Poe
Eleanor Roosevelt
Fidel Castro
George Lucas
George W. Bush
Gloria Estefan
Jack London
Jacques Cousteau
Jane Austen
Jesse Owens
Jesse Ventura
Jimi Hendrix
John Glenn
Latin Sensations
Legends of Dracula

Legends of Santa Claus
Louisa May Alcott
Madeleine Albright
Malcolm X
Mark Twain
Maya Angelou
Mohandas Gandhi
Mother Teresa
Nelson Mandela
Oprah Winfrey
Osama bin Laden
Princess Diana
Queen Cleopatra
Queen Elizabeth I
Queen Latifah
Rosie O'Donnell
Saddam Hussein
Saint Joan of Arc
Thurgood Marshall
Tiger Woods
Tony Blair
Vladimir Putin
William Shakespeare
Wilma Rudolph
Women in Space
Women of the Wild West
Yasser Arafat

ABOUT THE AUTHOR

JoAnn Bren Guernsey is the author of several young adult novels and many nonfiction titles. Her work has won several awards and in 2003 she received a McKnight Artist Fellowship in Prose from the Loft Literary Center. JoAnn lives in Minneapolis, Minnesota.

PHOTO ACKNOWLEDGMENTS

Photographs used with the permission of: © Jim Bourg/ Reuters/CORBIS, p. 2; © Reuters/CORBIS, pp. 6, 86, 98; © Time Life Pictures/Getty Images p. 10; Ernest Ricketts, p. 15; Martin Luther King Jr. Center for Nonviolent Social Change, Inc., p. 17; Maine South High School, pp. 18, 22, 54; © David J. & Janice L. Frent Collection/CORBIS, p. 19; © Brooks Kraft/CORBIS, pp. 25, 32; © Bettmann/CORBIS, pp. 27, 30; © Lee Balterman/Time Life Pictures/Getty Images, p. 34; © Brooke Shearer, p. 37; © Independent Picture Service, p. 39; © David Hume/Kennerly/Getty Images, p. 42; © 1974 by Hot Springs High School/ZUMA Press, p. 44; Arkansas Democrat Gazette, p. 48; © AP/Wide World Photos, pp. 50, 78; © Jon Levy/Liaison/Getty Images, p. 58; © Joseph Sohm; ChromoSohm Inc./CORBIS, p. 60; © Cynthia Johnson/Time Life Pictures/Getty Images, pp. 61, 71; © Peter Turnley/CORBIS, p. 62; The White House, p. 64; © Karl Gehring/Liaison/Getty Images, p. 80; © Jonathan Alcorn/ZUMA Press, p. 82; © Vivian Ronay/Liaison/Getty Images, p. 84; © Ken Lambert/Washington Times via Newsmakers/Getty Images, p. 88; © SZENES JASON/ CORBIS SYGMA, pp. 90, 94; © ELLIS RICHARD/CORBIS SYGMA, p. 93; © AHMAD MASOOD/Reuters/CORBIS, p. 101; © Peter Kramer/Getty Images, p. 103; © JASON REED/Reuters/ CORBIS, p. 104.

Cover photos (hard cover and soft cover): front, © Dan Herrick/ ZUMA Press; back, © STEWART MIKE/CORBIS SYGMA.